How Things Are Made

Tomatoes to Ketchup

By Inez Snyder

Children's Press®
A Division of Scholastic Inc.
New York / Toronto / London / Auckland / Sydney
Mexico City / New Delhi / Hong Kong
Danbury, Connecticut

Photo Credits: Cover and all photos by Maura B. McConnell
Contributing Editor: Jennifer Silate
Book Design: Mindy Liu

Library of Congress Cataloging-in-Publication Data

Snyder, Inez.
   Tomatoes to ketchup / by Inez Snyder.
   p. cm. — (How things are made)
   Includes index.
   Summary: Simple text and illustrations show how a mother and son cook
   tomatoes with vinegar and spices to make ketchup.
   ISBN 0-516-24266-0 (lib. bdg.) — ISBN 0-516-24358-6 (pbk.)
   1. Cookery (Ketchup)—Juvenile literature. 2. Cookery
   (Tomatoes)—Juvenile literature. 3. Tomatoes—Juvenile literature. [1.
   Ketchup.] I. Title. II. Series.

TX819.K48 S66 2003
641.8'14—dc21

                                                    2002008182

Contents

My name is Brian.

My mom and I are going to make **ketchup**.

5

We have to use a lot of tomatoes to make ketchup.

First, Mom cuts the tomatoes.

7

Next, I help put the
tomatoes in a pot.

Mom puts **vinegar**
in the pot, too.

9

Mom puts the pot
on the stove.

She puts the lid on the pot.

Now, the tomatoes
and vinegar must cook.

The tomatoes have cooked
for a long time.

Mom **pours** the vinegar
out of the pot.

Next, Mom puts **spices** in the pot.

She **stirs** the spices and the tomatoes together.

15

The ketchup must
cook longer.

Mom stirs it some more.

The ketchup is done.

Mom pours it into a jar.

I put ketchup on some **french fries**.

It tastes good!

21

New Words

french fries (**french friez**) strips of potato that are cooked in a pan with hot oil

ketchup (**kech**-uhp) a thick, red sauce that is made with tomatoes, vinegar, and spices

pours (**porz**) making something flow down and out of a container

spices (**spisse**-uhz) substances with special smells or tastes used to flavor food

stirs (**stuhrz**) mixing something by moving it around in a container with a spoon or a stick

vinegar (**vin**-uh-gur) a sour liquid used to flavor and preserve food

To Find Out More

Books
I Like Ketchup Sandwiches
by Lisa Conway
Random House, Incorporated

Tomato
by Barrie Watts
Silver Burdett Press

Web Site
Heinzsteinz Kids' Page
http://www.heinzflavor.com/kids/heinsteins.asp
This Web site has lots of ketchup information and recipes.

Index

french fries, 20

ketchup, 4, 6,
16, 18, 20

pours, 12, 18

spices, 14
stirs, 14, 16

tomatoes, 6, 8,
10, 12, 14

vinegar, 8, 10,
12

About the Author
Inez Snyder writes and edits children's books. She also enjoys painting and cooking for her family.

Reading Consultants

Kris Flynn, Coordinator, Small School District Literacy, The San Diego County Office of Education

Shelly Forys, Certified Reading Recovery Specialist, W.J. Zahnow Elementary School, Waterloo, IL

Sue McAdams, Former President of the North Texas Reading Council of the IRA, and Early Literacy Consultant, Dallas, TX